A LITTLE EARLY LEARNING POEM BOOK ABOUT THE LETTER G

A Little Early Learning Poem Book about the Letter G

Walter the Educator

Silent King Books

SILENT KING BOOKS

SKB

Copyright © 2024 by Walter the Educator

All rights reserved. No part of this book may be reproduced in any manner whatsoever without written permission except in the case of brief quotations embodied in critical articles and reviews.

First Printing, 2024

Disclaimer
This book is a literary work; poems are not about specific persons, locations, situations, and/or circumstances unless mentioned in a historical context. This book is for entertainment and informational purposes only. The author and publisher offer this information without warranties expressed or implied. No matter the grounds, neither the author nor the publisher will be accountable for any losses, injuries, or other damages caused by the reader's use of this book. The use of this book acknowledges an understanding and acceptance of this disclaimer.

dedicated to all the early learners across the world

THE LETTER G

In the land of words where stories dance,

There lives a letter in a whimsical trance.

It's none other than the grand and gallant G,

A hero of the alphabet, bold and free.

G is for giggles, gleeful and bright,

For the gentle breeze that kisses goodnight.

It's for the graceful glide of a butterfly,

And the glorious sun that lights up the sky.

In gardens, greenery grows with grace,

Where giggling geese gather in the space.

Grapes glisten in the golden sun's gleam,

And gentle giants graze, living the dream.

G is for the galaxy, vast and grand,

Where glittering stars in galaxies stand.

For the gentle waves that greet the shore,

And the gentle giants that forever soar.

In the realm of G, games galore,

With gleeful laughter, they explore.

They gallop like gazelles, so grand,

And play with gusto, hand in hand.

G is for the gems that gleam and glow,

And the gentle rain that helps them grow.

For the giggles of a baby's glee,

And the gift of friendship, pure and free.

In the garden, greenery thrives,

As G's grace in every leaf arrives.

With every gust, the grasses sway,

In the golden light of a gentle day.

G is for the giants, guardians tall,

Who watch over creatures, big and small.

With gentle hearts and generous hands,

They protect the precious, pristine lands.

In the galaxy, galaxies twirl,

With glittering stars that endlessly swirl.

In the gentle embrace of cosmic grace,

Glimmering galaxies find their place.

G is for the goodness we all share,

For the generosity beyond compare.

It's for the gratitude we hold dear,

And the gentle whispers we long to hear.

So let us gather in a grand parade,

In the glorious sunshine's golden cascade.

With giggles and games, we'll gallivant,

In the garden of G, forever enchant.

For G is a letter so grand and true,

In its gentle embrace, dreams renew.

So let us cherish each glorious day,

In the land of G, where wonders play.

ABOUT THE CREATOR

Walter the Educator is one of the pseudonyms for Walter Anderson. Formally educated in Chemistry, Business, and Education, he is an educator, an author, a diverse entrepreneur, and he is the son of a disabled war veteran. "Walter the Educator" shares his time between educating and creating. He holds interests and owns several creative projects that entertain, enlighten, enhance, and educate, hoping to inspire and motivate you.

> Follow, find new works, and stay up to date with Walter the Educator™ at WaltertheEducator.com

www.ingramcontent.com/pod-product-compliance
Lightning Source LLC
LaVergne TN
LVHW052004060526
838201LV00059B/3839